DITCH THE DAILY LESSON PLAN

How do I plan for meaningful student learning?

Michael
FISHER

ASCD   Alexandria, VA USA

ASCD | arias™

Website: www.ascd.org   www.ascdarias.org
E-mail: books@ascd.org

Copyright © 2015 by ASCD. All rights reserved. It is illegal to reproduce copies of this work in print or electronic format (including reproductions displayed on a secure intranet or stored in a retrieval system or other electronic storage device from which copies can be made or displayed) without the prior written permission of the publisher. Readers who wish to duplicate material copyrighted by ASCD may do so for a small fee by contacting the Copyright Clearance Center (CCC), 222 Rosewood Dr., Danvers, MA 01923, USA (phone: 978-750-8400; fax: 978-646-8600; Web: www.copyright.com). To inquire about site licensing options or any other reuse, contact ASCD Permissions at www.ascd.org/permissions, permissions@ascd.org, or 703-575-5749. Send translation inquiries to translations@ascd.org.

Printed in the United States of America. Cover art © 2015 by ASCD. ASCD publications present a variety of viewpoints. The views expressed or implied in this book should not be interpreted as official positions of the Association.

ASCD LEARN TEACH LEAD®, ASCD ARIAS™, and ANSWERS YOU NEED FROM VOICES YOU TRUST® are trademarks owned by ASCD and may not be used without permission. Triptik® is a registered trademark of the American Automobile Association. All other referenced trademarks are the property of their respective owners.

PAPERBACK ISBN: 978-1-4166-2169-0   ASCD product # SF116036

Also available as an e-book (see Books in Print for the ISBNs).

Library of Congress Cataloging-in-Publication Data
Names: Fisher, Mike.
Title: Ditch the daily lesson plan : how do I plan for meaningful student
    learning? / Mike Fisher.
Description: Alexandria, Virginia : ASCD, [2015] | Includes
bibliographical
    references.
Identifiers: LCCN 2015036674 | ISBN 9781416621690 (pbk.)
Subjects: LCSH: Curriculum planning. | Lesson planning.
Classification: LCC LB2806.15 .F55 2015 | DDC 375/.001--dc23 LC
record available at http://lccn.loc.gov/2015036674

24 23 22 21 20 19 18 17 16 15   1 2 3 4 5 6 7 8 9 10

DITCH THE DAILY LESSON PLAN

How do I plan for meaningful student learning?

Want to earn a free ASCD Arias e-book?
Your opinion counts! Please take 2–3 minutes to give
us your feedback on this publication. All survey
respondents will be entered into a drawing to
win an ASCD Arias e-book.

Please visit
www.ascd.org/ariasfeedback

Thank you!

Introduction

Early in my teaching career, I shared with a colleague my frustration that although I was teaching according to my lesson plan, my students didn't seem to be learning anything. My colleague gave me some of the best educational advice I'd ever get: "Slow down." At the time, I protested that slowing down seemed like an impossible option; I only had a certain amount of time before I had to administer a test, and I had all the steps leading up to the test neatly laid out in daily plans.

"Slow down," repeated my colleague. "If it's worth doing, then it's worth doing right."

Slowing down meant amending my plans and trying to figure out what the learning priorities were. I was overwhelmed by the colossal responsibility of all that was necessary to have students learn while they were with me.

In their book *Pyramid Response to Intervention* (2009), authors Buffum, Mattos, and Weber posit the following formula: instruction plus time equals learning. If instruction and instructional time were both constant, we might reason that learning levels would also be constant. But we know that not all students learn at the same rate—variability is built into the system. Because of this, we need to reframe the conversation about how students learn. If learning is variable while instruction and instructional time remain constant, then how can teachers help students to learn more?

The answer is simple: They must shake up the equation. Both instruction and instructional time need to be variable so that learning becomes constant. That's the sweet spot, and that's what I'm targeting in this book. How can we build variability of instruction and instructional time into the system to strategically plan for meaningful student learning?

Ditch The Daily Lesson Plan

What we used to do as educators worked when we were simply preparing kids for industry and there were few opportunities for them to leave their hometowns. Now that we're preparing kids for jobs that don't yet exist and opportunities that are limited only by ambition, the time has come for us to modernize our teaching methods. Instructional nostalgia won't work anymore. "The way we've always done it" is no longer an option.

It's time to ditch the daily lesson plan.

I often say in workshops that teachers should stop creating "plans" and start designing lesson "events" or "experiences." Events and experiences help students develop an emotional attachment to their learning that in turn translates into strong memories—and lessons that are memorable are lessons that will stick.

What do you remember about your school experiences? The worksheets you filled out? The comprehension questions at the end of each chapter you read? The lectures? No? What about those moments that departed from the routine? What about the field trips you took, or that time your teacher dressed up as Jon Bon Jovi and sang the periodic table of elements to the tune of "You Give Love A Bad Name?" That which is memorable sticks.

Some Caveats

I have several colleagues who are concerned with my stance on instruction. As one critical friend bluntly put it, "If you're going to propose that teachers ditch lesson planning, then their decision to do so must be rooted in their experiences with the process. No time will be saved and no depth will be gained if they just jump to a more sophisticated version of lesson or curriculum design without first understanding the nuances of day-to-day classroom and curriculum management."

Touché. I don't disagree. But once teachers internalize those nuances, then it's time to start ditching some tradition—without necessarily ditching planning wholesale. In their ASCD Arias *Solving 25 Problems in Unit Design* (2015), authors McTighe and Wiggins note that "teachers often design jam-packed units . . . that leave little or no time allotted to address the inevitable setbacks and unexpected interruptions" that are bound to occur (p. 43). They describe scenarios in which teachers with too much content to cover try to maximize class time by teaching everything that needs to be taught rather than focusing on the learning that's happening. When we boil what we do down to intentional actions, are we more concerned with planning the lessons or planning for learning? I'm not saying that structure doesn't matter; I am saying that planning and documentation matter, just not in the way we've always done it. Contemporary curriculum design requires us to understand the strategic decisions that we must make to meet our students' learning needs.

Lesson planning in and of itself is not a bad practice, but it's outdated. Figure 1 shows the difference between a traditional approach to planning lessons and the more contemporary approach that I advocate here.

FIGURE 1: **Traditional vs. Contemporary Lesson Planning**

Traditional Lesson Planning	Contemporary Lesson Planning
Teachers plan individual daily lessons down to the details, including the amount of time allotted for discrete objectives. Planning is ongoing throughout the year.	Teachers largely exclude details and put in more work upfront to minimize planning throughout the year (except for tweaks in response to student learning).
Lesson content depends largely on the length of classes, and the amount of time planned and allotted for teaching (either by the teacher or by an outside resource such as a textbook).	Lessons are open-ended while also including planned instructional milestones or student-navigated checkpoints and resources.

Teachers document the same types of elements (e.g., objectives, standards, procedures, resources) on each daily lesson plan.	Teachers document objectives, standards, procedures, resources, and so on only once, at the beginning of the year.
Students have few opportunities to engage in discovery while learning due to time limitations.	Students have many opportunities to engage in discovery while learning.
Lessons often rely heavily on outside resources that dictate the time allotted for teaching specific content.	Lessons engage students' skills through multiple dynamic resources that change from year to year and that students have a hand in selecting.
Lessons are tightly structured and offer little time for teachers and students to go deeper into the content. Teachers will often address contingencies outside of class time (such as after school or in the form of homework assignments) to ensure that daily lesson plans aren't disrupted.	Lessons build in time for students to explore content deeply and continue developing their skills so that they can be prepared for the next learning moment.

One of the big benefits of ditching the daily lesson plan is the permission it gives us to rethink the *what* of lessons and redouble our efforts around the *how* and the *why*. It allows us to take risks with content, encourage meaningful explorations, and reimagine teaching and learning for the modern age.

In their book *Learning Personalized* (2015), authors Zmuda, Curtis, and Ullman ask, "How do we reconceptualize learning to move beyond passive student roles of recording and recalling because the world beyond the school walls demands adaptive, creative problem solvers?" (p. 6). If the world is demanding adaptive and creative problem solvers, how does ensuring that all content is covered in a down-to-the-minute plan help students? I don't think it does. I believe we need to think differently about curriculum design and planning efforts. I want teachers to use their time wisely while developing contemporary habits around curriculum design that focus more on the learning and the learner than on strict adherence to a plan.

Now, let's take a look at some varied ways to accomplish this.

The Mini Unit

Almost all types of lesson plans share certain core elements: an objective; suggested lengths of time for supported practice, independent practice, and wrapping up the lesson; and information about differentiated practices or other special considerations to reach all learners.

I propose embracing a more sophisticated version of lesson planning that focuses on elements that overlap across multiple daily lesson plans. What are the similarities or redundancies in the system? What new information is valuable? What is worth recording or documenting? If you're using a lesson plan template, you still can—you'll just be recording actions across multiple days rather than for each individual lesson.

Here's an example of the elements for a modern, time-saving lesson that places learners at the center. The plan is for a 1st grade "Mini Unit" on geometry and the exploration of shapes and their attributes.

Overview and Objectives

Based on the three Common Core Standards for geometry, students should be able to

- Identify basic shapes.
- Distinguish between defining and non-defining attributes.
- Build and draw shapes with defining attributes.
- Build and draw two- and three-dimensional shapes.
- Compose and decompose circles and rectangles into two and four equal shares.
- Describe the shares of decomposed shapes using appropriate math terms.

Standards

- *CCSS.MATH.1.G.A.1:* Distinguish between defining attributes (e.g., triangles are closed and three-sided) versus non-defining attributes (e.g., color, orientation, overall size); build and draw shapes to possess defining attributes.

- *CCSS.MATH.1.G.A.2:* Compose two-dimensional shapes (rectangles, squares, trapezoids, triangles, half-circles, and quarter-circles) or three-dimensional shapes (cubes, right rectangular prisms, right circular cones, and right circular cylinders) to create a composite shape, and compose new shapes from the composite shape.
- *CCSS.MATH.1.G.A.3:* Partition circles and rectangles into two and four equal shares, describe the shares using the words halves, fourths, and quarters, and use the phrases half of, fourth of, and quarter of. Describe the whole as two of or four of the shares. Understand for these examples that decomposing into more equal shares creates smaller shares. (NGA & CCSSO, 2010)

Because the overview and objectives would be the same across this learning experience, teachers wouldn't need to document them every day—only once, in a single Mini Unit document. The same goes for other curricular elements, such as beginning- and closing-of-class procedures and sequence of instruction. By recording everything in one place, we negate the need to create and adhere to individual daily plans and can therefore focus on student learning instead.

The Mini Unit document is similar to an enhanced lesson plan or a short unit plan. In this model, the teacher works directly from the "Activities, Resources, and Assessments" section, which is separate from any curriculum tool. In our example, the arc of combined lessons leads us away from time-dependent and toward learning-dependent instructional actions:

Activities, Resources, and Assessments

- *Pre-assessment Check*: Read and discuss the book *Shapes*.
- Identify a variety of shapes using individual shape manipulatives, apps, or interactive whiteboards.
- Using appropriate math terms, students will demonstrate, alone and in groups, that they understand the names of the shapes and will begin discussing their attributes.
- Students will use pattern blocks, geo blocks, and geo boards to build and draw shapes, compose new shapes, and decompose existing ones.
- *Assessment*: Students will identify shapes and draw shapes. (All assessments in this lesson experience can take many forms: consultation, observation, review of performance on a device, and so on.)
- Students continue discussing the *Shapes* book as well as defining and non-defining attributes.
- Students use pattern blocks, geo blocks, and geo boards to compose or classify shapes by their attributes.
- Students sort their shapes according to various given attributes, explaining and defending their reasoning.

- *Assessment*: Students will identify shape attributes and, given a particular attribute, draw several shapes that match.
- Students will use two- and three-dimensional shapes to create composite shapes.
- Using circles and rectangles, the teacher will model and students will practice decomposing shapes by halves and fourths.
- *Assessment*: Students will decompose composite shapes into their components and circles and rectangles into halves and fourths.
- *End-of-Lesson-Experience Performance Task—The Attribute Museum*: Through drawing, digital illustration, or photography, students will individually find and contribute something in their environment that represents one of their learned shapes. They will label their contributions with their attributes, noting whether these are defining or non-defining, and perhaps with some information about their shapes when divided into halves, quarters, or smaller fractions. Students will then hang their contributions around the room and participate with teachers in conversations about the images using the "See, Think, and Wonder" thinking routine from Harvard's Project Zero. (See, Think, Wonder Thinking Routine, 2014)

Alternatively, the above section could easily be a list of instructional tasks, learning demonstrations, or checkpoints guiding the path that the learning experience will take. In our example, the teacher would want to add additional, more granular details to their plans, such as the following:

- The exact types of two- and three-dimensional shapes that they expect their students to learn
- Vocabulary processes for new words—perhaps paying special attention to roots, prefixes, and suffixes (e.g., teaching that the tri- in triangle means three)
- Specific assessment measures
- Scaffolds and differentiated practices, including how to group students in pairs or small groups
- Notes on concepts or activities that may be problematic for students and possible contingencies

It isn't necessary to adhere to a particular style of planning. Depending on your judgment and conversations with colleagues, you may want to include specific content knowledge and precise skill statements in your plan, or perhaps lists of any additional resources you might use. I didn't include any sort of anticipatory set or closure in my plan above; you might want to document some sort of spiral review, but that decision will depend on the lesson arc and should only be included in your plan as a function of conversation and consensus with your colleagues or administration.

Note that the plan in our example fits on about two and a half pages total versus a page or two per day. If you'd like to try implementing the Mini Unit model, keep in mind that in-the-moment formative assessments might reveal potential new activities, time adjustments, or paths of interest; pursuing these will make your teaching more responsive and professional dialogue around planning and reflection much richer.

I purposefully did not include deadlines in my plan. When learning happens and everyone is ready, that's when we move to the next task. Some students may hit the finish line ahead of the others and some may lag behind, so differentiating practice, scaffolding for success, and providing opportunities for enrichment and sophistication still matter a great deal.

In A Nutshell

The Mini Unit model saves time in a couple of ways. First, the teacher isn't creating a document every day, but relying instead on a single short, all-inclusive document for a weeks-long lesson or short unit. Second, the model encourages a more fluid learning process whereby learning and mastering moments lead seamlessly into one another. Depending on the differentiation methods employed, the Mini Unit model may actually help students learn faster than the traditional daily-planning model.

I believe the Mini Unit model is particularly good for building background knowledge and foundational skills. Although there is room for some discovery-level learning, much of the lesson is directed by the teacher. For a more expansive model, consider the Curriculum Cache.

The Curriculum Cache

An extension of the Mini Unit model is the Curriculum Cache model—an all-inclusive, one-stop shop for teaching. Many schools have curriculum maps or detailed units of study already in place that teachers use to create lesson plans. These are good starting points for creating a curriculum cache, but only if plans and maps are already aligned. Because we are going to be adding layers to already documented work, we want to make sure that we're working from a solid foundation. There are two main steps to creating a cache: strengthening and clarifying the current plan, and adding the elements necessary to eschew daily lesson plans.

To strengthen and clarify the plan, I recommend answering the following "C.L.E.A.R." questions:

- *Clarity*: How transparent is the plan's language? How transparent are your intentions as a teacher?
- *Liveliness*: Does the plan include contemporary and dynamic teaching methods, tools, and products?
- *Evidence*: Does the plan document evidence of learning in the included assessments and does the assessment evidence become more sophisticated over the course of the unit?
- *Alignment*: Does the plan show cohesion across content, skills, assessments, and cognition levels?

- *Robustness*: When adding components to the plan, do these further the robustness and rigor of teaching and learning?

These questions are not linear; they offer systemic opportunities rather than isolated improvement zones. Being clear when planning is essential to the big *C*s of curriculum work: conversation, collaboration, and consensus. Answering the above questions in the affirmative helps to ensure transparency, continued conversation about curriculum, and the natural evolution of the curriculum going forward.

Some unit plans already include activities and lists of potential resources. These are the elements we will target in the Curriculum Cache model. For the model to work, we need to consider which elements in the teaching and learning process are limited by time and which are limited by learning. We are seeking a sweet spot for actual learning here, not simply to cover what we need to cover in a 40-minute period.

For the cache, I propose referring to "activities" as "instructional actions" instead. Teachers will document activities they've agreed upon with colleagues as well as more nuanced actions for student practice and other fundamentals of the traditional lesson plan. You can think of the cache as a step-by-step plan of intentional actions including both what students will do and what they will learn. How will students navigate the ebb and flow of foundational information and demonstrate that they feel comfortable with it? How might they analyze or creatively address new knowledge? Investing time in answering these questions is one of the ways in which the Curriculum Cache model ultimately helps save teachers time. As with the Mini Unit, teachers can teach directly from the cache without translating the unit into individual daily moments.

I think it's fine for the cache to include detailed information on formative assessments, vocabulary instruction, scaffolding and differentiation strategies, homework, and so on. It's also fine to include some deadlines, such as expectations for reaching particular milestones by a given date.

Curriculum Cache Example: "Teenage Angst: How Teenagers Are Depicted in Popular Media"

Overview

Teenagers have unique characteristics. They are no longer children but also not yet adults. This unit is about exploring modern teen realities, such as how teens deal with the consequences of their actions. We will examine the teenage condition and how it is represented in popular music and other types of media.

Standards: Reading for Literature, 8th Grade
Key Ideas and Details

Standard 1: Cite the textual evidence that most strongly supports an analysis of what the text says explicitly as well as inferences drawn from the text.

Standard 2: Determine a theme or central idea of a text and analyze its development over the course of the text, including its relationship to the characters, setting, and plot; provide an objective summary of the text.

Craft and Structure
Standard 4: Determine the meaning of words and phrases as they are used in a text, including figurative and connotative meanings; analyze the impact of specific word choices on meaning and tone, including analogies or allusions to other texts.

Integration of Language and Ideas
Standard 7: Analyze the extent to which a filmed or live production of a story or drama stays faithful to or departs from the text or script, evaluating the choices made by the director or actors.

Standard 9: Analyze how a modern work of fiction draws on themes, patterns of events, or character types from myths, traditional stories, or religious works such as the Bible, including describing how the material is rendered new.

Standards: Writing, 8th Grade
Standard 6: Use technology, including the Internet, to produce and publish writing and present the relationships between information and ideas efficiently as well as to interact and collaborate with others.

Standard 7: Conduct short research projects to answer a question (including a self-generated question), drawing on several sources and generating additional related, focused questions that allow for multiple avenues of exploration.

Standard 9: Draw evidence from literary or informational texts to support analysis, reflection, and research. (NGA & CCSSO, 2010)

Big Ideas

- Effective readers compare and evaluate multiple types of media formats.
- Effective readers use appropriate details to support their inferences and conclusions.
- Determining a musician's purpose helps the reader better understand and interpret the lyrics.
- Attraction to a piece of music is grounded in one's experience (cultural background, life events), mood, and setting.

Essential Questions

- What is the text really about?
- How do I figure out the meanings of words or phrases?
- How does the way a song is sung affect the meaning of the lyrics?
- How does the way a song is visualized affect the meaning of the lyrics?
- What makes a lyric or a work of music memorable?

Content

- *Textual Analysis and Evidence for Thinking:* Themes and central ideas, inferencing, summarization

- *Comparative Analysis.* Multiple media types, multiple media treatment
- *Reflective Writing.* Text-based evidence, conclusions based on analysis and evidence
- *Publishing.* Digital format

Skills

- Cite, orally and in writing, evidence from text to support reasoning and conclusions based on an established or self-defined theme or central idea.
- Analyze in writing thematic elements in text (e.g., specific lines in lyrics).
- Infer the author's meaning, orally and in writing, based on textual evidence.
- Summarize, orally and in writing, key points in the text based on an established or self-defined theme or central idea.
- Compare and contrast—orally, in writing, and using digital tools—anchor text to supporting media, including similar-treatment text (e.g., music lyrics with a similar theme) and media representation of text (e.g., a music video), and justify reasoning using media-based evidence.
- Explain, in writing and using digital tools, the relevance of anchor-text content and evidence or lack thereof in supporting media.
- Reflect, in writing, on evidence garnered from both lyrics and supporting informational texts.

- Analyze the author's main idea both orally and in writing, drawing conclusions based on analysis of multiple texts and pieces of evidence.
- Analyze—orally, in writing, and using digital tools— multiple types of media to determine important information and connections among them.
- Digitally publish the most important information based on the parameters of the established task.
- Rationalize, in writing, the choice of Web 2.0 tools selected for publishing conclusions.

Vocabulary

Discuss any of the brand names and the words *postcode, envy, trippin'* (socially constructed definition), *timepiece,* and *luxe* from the lyrics to Lorde's "Royals" as well as any pertinent vocabulary from related texts. A process-oriented approach is expected, with students using the vocabulary in multiple interactions and the teacher holding them accountable for doing so. The teacher should seek to construct definitions socially when possible within authentic moments (i.e., when the word comes up naturally) and develop student understanding of the new words using explanations, visualizations, etymological analysis, games, and peer discussions.

Proposed Assessments

- *Mid-Unit Assessment 1:* Using their notes and recalling their conversations, students summarize their observations so far, including any supporting evidence.
- *Mid-Unit Assessment 2:* Students make a claim about teenagers that they can support with information they

collect from lyrics, videos, and supporting texts. They should use details from the various media to support their claim. Students should also include comparative and contrasting information from the media they've examined as well as a reflective statement about the relevance of the evidence to their work. Depending on the depth of student conversations and the constraints of time, the teacher may want to consider having students also address counter-claims in their writing.

- *Final Assessment:* Students create an infographic of their comparative analysis of song lyrics, music, videos, and supporting texts. Student can choose to use digital tools such as Piktochart, Glogster, or Smore to create their infographic. Students will submit their infographics either in print or online along with a reflective summary. (See instructional actions for more details.)

Proposed Instructional Actions
Part 1

- Introduce students to just the song lyrics.
- Students use the Notice, Think, and Wonder rubric (see link in Resources section on p. 25) to think about their first impressions of the lyrics.
- Discuss the main idea behind the lyrics. This step prepares students for close reading of the lyrics further in the lesson.
- *Engagement opportunity:* Students arrive at the main idea as a group, but then have to each individually

compose a tweet of 140 characters or fewer communicating important information. (This step helps students to prioritize information in chunks. Tweets could be posted around the room and class can discuss them during a "gallery walk.")

- Students discuss lyrical themes (e.g., innocence lost, fate, inability to control the world at large).
- Students brainstorm ways to represent the lyrics visually.
- Students create a video presentation of the lyrics digitally, using software such as iMovie, Windows Movie Maker, or any number of apps available online.
- Students share their presentations with peers and collect evidence about connections among them using two-column paper and the Notice, Think, and Wonder rubric.
- Students work through a close reading of the lyrics over the course of a day or two (or however long it takes).
- Students write a paragraph or two describing evidence of the main idea. (Possible prompt: "How does the author develop the central idea over the course of these lyrics?")
- *Engagement Opportunity:* Students' engage in a further close reading of the lyrics by reviewing the annotated version at rock.genius.com. (This could double as an opportunity for further writing and connecting if students add their own annotations.)
- Students participate in a close viewing of the music video with the volume turned down.

- *Scaffolding Opportunity:* Students compare and contrast videos and lyrics using a 3-D Graphic organizer from the Brainigami LiveBinder (www.livebinders.com) and brainstorm visuals that exemplify similarities and differences.
- Using the Notice, Think, and Wonder rubric, students engage in peer discussions about each other's discoveries and evidence. Discussions can either be teacher-guided or conducted in small groups.
- *Mid-point Assessment*: Students summarize their observations and discoveries so far.

Part 2

- *Engagement Opportunity:* Students share one big discovery or connection that they've made in a collaborative Google Doc. In a whole-class discussion, students then look for overlaps in thinking and "aha!" moments that they may not have previously considered.
- Students read one or more of the comparative texts, annotating them first as individuals and then as a group. (See the Annotexting LiveBinder link in the Resources section on p. 25.)
- Students return to the original lyrics and look for additional connections that would be useful in a comparative analysis.
- Students ask and answer text-dependent questions that lead them to a main idea or relationship and cull evidence for their thinking from multiple sources.

- *Additional Midpoint Assessment:* Students make a claim about teenagers that they can support with information they've collected from the lyrics, videos, and supporting texts. They should use details from the various media to support their claim.

Part 3

- Students brainstorm potential school-appropriate songs or videos that exemplify the teenage condition.
- The teacher introduces students to infographics and tools for creating them, perhaps through mini-lessons or by asking savvy students to teach the other students about them.
- *Potential Scaffold:* Students read and respond in writing to articles about teenagers using the song they've selected for comparison.
- *Final Assessment:* Students create their infographics using evidence from at least one other source to comparatively analyze their chosen song.
- Students write a reflective piece noting their decision-making rationales, their thoughts about the song they chose, and what it is about the song that makes it a memorable work of art.
- Using a co-created rubric, students assess each other's work.
- *Potential Assessment Upgrade*: Students publish their work online and solicit feedback from students somewhere else in the world. Students use the

feedback to tweak their infographics before turning them in for final publication on the teacher's website.

Resources

- "Royals" video: http://bit.ly/1hhn58f. Note that this video is slightly different from the official U.S. version available here: http://bit.ly/1jAPuck. Consider extending the work with close viewings and comparative analysis of the two versions.
- Close reading document: http://bit.ly/1N1UZPr
- Close viewing document: http://bit.ly/1MhxC5U
- Potential comic relief: Weird Al Yankovic's Parody of "Royals," "Foil": http://bit.ly/1naOPIO
- Annotated "Royals" lyrics at Rock Genius: http://genius.com/Lorde-royals-lyrics
- Notice, Think, and Wonder rubric: http://bit.ly/1Mhy0Be
- Brainigami LiveBinder: http://www.livebinders.com/play/play?id=375487
- Annotexting LiveBinder: http://www.livebinders.com/play/play?id=322571
- Article on the Notice, Think, and Wonder rubric in *In Transition Journal* (p. 15): http://bit.ly/1OnVkPC
- List of infographics resources: http://bit.ly/1Rw9rR6

Potential Supporting or Comparative Texts

- "16 Teens Arrested after Tweeting Party": http://huff.to/1Gyr5gR
- "The Bling Ring": http://en.wikipedia.org/wiki/Bling_Ring
- "Who Are the Millenials?": http://www.livescience.com/38061-millennials-generation-y.html
- "The Selfie Syndrome": http://on.today.com/1FUWcIR
- "When Everybody Gets a Trophy, Nobody Wins": http://huff.to/1jdcEcJ

I think it would also be a good idea if, a year down the road, all of the resources in the cache were replaced. Keep them aligned to the standards, keep the content, skills, and most of the assessments, and throw everything else out. Freshen up the cache with new media, new supporting texts, and perhaps an upgraded final assessment featuring whatever's hot in technology. Augmented reality? Game simulation? Multimedia presentation played on students' t-shirts with built-in adaptive projectors? (Kidding, but wouldn't that be cool?)

In A Nutshell

As with the Mini Unit model, the Curriculum Cache contains all of the elements of a unit and detailed instructional actions so that it doesn't need to be translated into individual daily plans. Where the Mini Unit model is good for building background knowledge, the Curriculum Cache model is better suited for exploration and creativity on the part of students. The model also saves teachers planning time while increasing student learning time and engagement.

When designing the cache, I recommend collaborating with colleagues to identify opportunities for content and resource integration, and to discuss priorities in standards and assessments. Though the cache shown here includes three "Instructional Actions" sections, it would be perfectly appropriate to streamline them or even remove one altogether if time constraints are a factor. Just keep in mind that the focus should be on learning and not whether or not you can fit certain actions into a particular amount of time. Instruction should always be planned to meet the learning needs of the students, not the timing needs of the teacher.

The Triptik® Model

In the late 1970s, I remember going on road trips with my parents and using the Triptik maps from the American Automobile Association (AAA). These were more than just maps—they also included information about road construction, speed limits, attractions, and events that were occurring at the time of our trip. In order to get a Triptik, one of my parents had to call an AAA representative and provide some basic information: the destination, certainly, as well as the dates of our trip, and any particular routes, points of interest and stopping points that we might wish to explore.

Of course, nowadays you can get instant travel information from AAA or any number of online travel sites. But when I was a kid, it was really exciting waiting for the Triptik to arrive and then poring over the maps and associated information when it did. I think this is a fabulous metaphor for unit design—particularly when we invite students to the table and let them help determine what their instructional path will be. We still set a destination, but the students help decide how we get there. We might coach the students in essential elements, anchor questions, and common assessment moments, but it's the students, engaging in constant inquiry across the course of the unit, who themselves discover what they need to learn.

The value of the Triptik model is in its scope, as it requires a breadth of authentic resources, and in the fact that the information within it is dynamic enough that iterations of the trip could differ greatly while still arriving at the same destination.

Unlike the Mini Unit and Curriculum Cache models, the Triptik model isn't dependent on a curriculum that is already in place. This model is particularly effective for brand-new unit plans and provides an opportunity for integrated content and contemporary instructional practices with new skills and tools. The model is predicated on the following criteria:

1. Finding a worthy learning journey on which to embark

2. Aligning the destination to standards, assessments, and perhaps variable products across multiple media types

3. Setting the essential skills

4. Focusing the work for the team by developing both essential and supporting questions

5. Co-creating with students tentative instructional tasks based on skills and strategies for getting to the assessment

It is important to be mindful of the destination while working to reach it by setting instructional milestones and providing ongoing feedback to students.

The following is an example of the Triptik model.

Step 1: Find a Worthy Journey

Eleventh grade earth science students in Texas are concerned about earthquakes that the media says may be related to increased fracking activities in their area. Students want to learn more about fracking and its environmental impact so that they can create a report or presentation for their local city council, which provides permits for companies engaged in the practice.

Step 2: Align the Destination

First, align the destination to assessment: students want to create a report or presentation communicating what they've discovered in their research. As they collect their data, students will need to make strategic decisions about what to focus on. Students should coach them through their curations and be able to reflect on the relevance of their resources.

Then, align the destination to standards: The Texas Essential Knowledge and Skills (TEKS) standards for science include several opportunities for alignment to the destination:

- *112.36 (b)(4) Science and social ethics:* Scientific decision making is a way of answering questions about the natural world. Students should be able to distinguish between scientific decision-making methods and ethical and social decisions that involve the application of scientific information.

- *112.36 (b)(6)(C) Relevance:* The interacting components of Earth's system change by both natural and human-influenced processes. Natural processes include hazards such as flooding, earthquakes, volcanoes, hurricanes, meteorite impacts, and climate change. Some human-influenced processes such as pollution and nonsustainable use of Earth's natural resources may damage Earth's system. Examples include climate change, soil erosion, air and water pollution, and biodiversity loss. The time scale of these changes and their impact on human society must be understood to make wise decisions concerning the use of the land, water, air, and natural resources. Proper stewardship of Earth will prevent unnecessary degradation and destruction of Earth's subsystems and diminish detrimental impacts to individuals and society.

- *112.36 (c) (3) Scientific processes:* The student uses critical thinking, scientific reasoning, and problem solving to make informed decisions within and outside the classroom.

- *112.36 (c) (12) Solid Earth:* The student knows that Earth contains energy, water, mineral, and rock resources and that use of these resources affects Earth's subsystems. (Texas Education Agency, 2007)

The above standards are only examples. There will be many opportunities for aligning the destination to other content areas, such as English language arts, or to established measures (e.g., Partnership for 20th Century Learning skills, ISTE standards).

Alignment to standards might invite further conversations about setting essential skills, integrating instruction across content areas, and, eventually, creating an action plan for even greater depth.

Step 3: Set Essential Skills

Skills can be dictated both by the established assessment and by the standards. In terms of assessment, students must certainly be able to draw conclusions from their research and create a presentation that represents their data, but if they're creating a detailed presentation, a written report isn't necessary. In terms of standards, students should be able to distinguish among scientific methods and their applications to ethical and social decisions. They must research and justify their resources and the data they chose to analyze regarding the interacting components of Earth's systems as it relates to their learning destination. Students must think critically and use reasoning and problem-solving skills to make informed decisions and they must be able to apply their knowledge of resources to the effect of fracking on the environment.

Step 4: Focus on the Work

Students work with the teacher to develop questions to both guide students through the inquiry process and develop content knowledge per the standards:

- Why does knowledge of humans' effect on the environment matter?
- What is fracking?
- What are the benefits and disadvantages of fracking?
- Why is our area conducive to fracking activities?
- What studies have been done on the possible connection between fracking and earthquakes?
- What did those studies find?
- What recommendations might we make based on science?
- What recommendations might we make based on social or ethical considerations?
- Does our area currently benefit from fracking?
- What are some long-term issues associated with fracking?

Some of these are essential questions, others are supporting questions, and the list is by no means exhaustive—it will grow considerably as the work gets underway. During this step, it might be a good idea to upgrade the work by creating a digital question bank using tools such as Google Docs or Today's Meet. It is important for the development of students' critical thinking and inquiry skills that they collate, sort, sift, and group the questions, curating the list to best suit their work. Asking and answering the right questions will help focus the inquiry, or maybe lead students in a new and previously unplanned direction—an awesome result itself!

Step 5: Co-Create Tentative Tasks

The main performance task for this lesson experience will be in the form of a presentation to the local city council. Leading up to that point, students and the teacher will want to set instructional parameters as though they were an action planning committee. Here are some categories of questions they might consider:

- *Role:* Who's doing what in the research process?
- *Orbits:* Who else might need to be involved? In our example, possibilities might include a technology teacher, an ELA teacher, scientists, or news organizations.
- *Tasks:* What learning journey will students embark on before the next meeting? How will they prepare for the meeting?
- *Feedback:* How will students give and receive feedback? How will the feedback guide their ongoing journey?
- *Limiting Factors:* when will students need to diverge from their original plan? What parameters might they need to alter? How will divergence affect the destination? What additional questions should we be asking?

It is with complete intention that the above categories create the acronym ROTFL—internet lingo for "rolling on the floor laughing." I thought that students would get a kick out of the novelty, and the acronym serves as a reminder that learning is meant to be fun and engaging. (If that's a little too cheesy for your taste, feel free to switch up the order of categories.)

Step 6: Be Mindful of the Destination

In our example, all of the shared decision-making tasks are focused on creating a quality presentation about fracking. Students will be learning planned-for skills around content as well as researching information and developing additional skills to create a quality presentation. Students must become masters of the knowledge they seek and demonstrate different ways to apply and evaluate that knowledge. The teacher's role as coach here is extremely important.

The Triptik model is less about content delivery than it is about access to information and content discovery. It will involve helping students curate resources and ask questions that focus the task and reminding students often about their end goal.

Ongoing feedback is extremely important, but it doesn't necessarily have to come from the teacher; it can come from anyone in the students' learning "orbit"—that is, anyone involved in the learning process. Feedback should be focused on improving the work and guiding students toward the final product. Students can use the feedback in multiple ways, from setting small goals (e.g., developing more questions) to establishing larger instructional milestones (e.g., committing to using a digital tool for the presentation and creating an accompanying outline to help guide content and performance decisions).

In A Nutshell

In the Triptik model, time for planning is built into the work with the students. Though the teacher may have some standards in mind, the actual plan for learning and discovery is co-created with students during class time. In short, the model requires little advance preparation beyond having a topic or theme in mind, an understanding of the relevant standards, and a willingness to relinquish some of the design control to students. The actual completion of the performance task may take some time depending on resources, amount of collaboration, understanding of the concepts involved or the digital tools used, and so on. Deadlines may need to be negotiated to keep the journey from becoming a lengthy unit, and the teacher must monitor students to ensure that they complete their research and presentation in a timely manner.

This model offers a good opportunity for enlisting the help of other teachers and adding them to the "orbit" as integrated partners in inquiry. Doing so can allow students to work on their journey in multiple places at multiple times.

Breaking the Mold

How much of what teachers do is either out of habit or due to an administrative mandate? I personally know principals with stacks of lesson plans in their office closets or vaults that have been there for years as nothing more than evidence that teachers do what they are told to do. If William Butler Yeats is correct and "education is the lighting of a fire," I know where to find the kindling.

It's 2015. What have we learned about effective curriculum design, and what are we holding onto as stalwarts of practice that help us cover what we have to cover but don't necessarily help us to uncover what really matters—authentic student learning?

In order for ditching daily lesson plans to work, everybody needs to be on board. Buy-in matters very much here. Everybody involved needs to have a high degree of trust in the system and be working toward a common goal. That means that there are some things that we need to let go of and other things we need to embrace.

As I wrap up, I'd like to mention the importance of vision and trust. One of the most important recommendations of the Interstate School Leaders Licensure Consortium (ISLLC) policy standards is to nurture and sustain "a culture of collaboration, trust, learning, and high expectations" (2008). The most important element of a successful culture is learning, followed closely by trust. There's been a huge loss of trust in education in the last few years and it's beginning to negatively affect student learning.

Curriculum is not a pizza delivered; it is a pizza made, with quality ingredients and creative recipes. We need to take back ownership of curriculum design rather than trusting blindly in big wallets and salesmen. A suit can't give us what we need. Teachers are perfectly capable of doing this work. But there has to be a change in school culture for them to do so successfully. We trust teachers with children but not with curriculum decisions? Come on.

Contingencies crop up in the teaching process—but so do opportunities for greater depth and creativity. In order for learning to be constant, remember that we have to allow variability in the process. Negotiating every minute doesn't really matter; it's reaching the destination that does.

It's time to liberate yourself and ditch the daily lesson plan. It's time to reflect on the joys of teaching through the lens of the contemporary educator and your contemporary learners. It's time to make bold moves and take classroom risks and reimagine how we do school. It's time to plan for more meaningful student learning.

Ditch the daily lesson plan—but don't ditch good planning.

To give your feedback on this publication and
be entered into a drawing for a free ASCD
Arias e-book, please visit
www.ascd.org/ariasfeedback

ENCORE

OTHER STUFF TO DITCH

Ditch the textbook or dependency on a resource. If I had a nickel for every time someone told me that they didn't need plans or units or maps because the product they were using already had them laid out, I would be a very rich man. Every resource is ephemeral: there one day, gone the next. And resource vendors don't know your students; they focus on a generalized middle ground. It's like having a lifeguard who only watches the middle of a pool. Teachers who make decisions about what to cut, keep, or create around their instructional practice or who design their own curriculum altogether have a much deeper understanding of the intricate interconnections among all of the elements of a well-designed curriculum. A well-designed curriculum rooted in standards with powerful content and well-defined skills allows for a revolving door of resources meaningful to students that may change from year to year depending on the students' needs.

Ditch the Internet filters. Limiting access online limits learning. Students should be protected from bad things, but not all things. Today's students are more likely to search YouTube for instructions on something than they are to Google it. Teachers should be able to get around any filter if they deem a website fit for learning. (Per CIPA rules, "An authorized person may disable the blocking or filtering measure during use by an adult to enable access for bona fide research or other lawful purposes" [2001].) The section on college and career capacities at the beginning of the main Common Core document states that students should "use technology and digital media strategically and capably" (NGA & CCSSO, 2015). How can students act strategically if they don't have access to all the potential learning resources online (including social media sites, which are almost always blocked in schools)? How can they act capably if they are limited to a very few tools that matter only in school but don't really prepare them for using the Web in the outside world? Filtering limits collaboration opportunities, amplified problem solving, and global connections. School is still a place for learning, right?

Ditch the no-cellphone policy. We have the ability to enable learning everywhere with devices that students tend to carry with them. I realize that there are issues of equity involved—not all students can afford cellphones, but these devices are the new pencils and should be as readily available to students. Should their use be managed? Yes. Should it be micro-managed? No. Figure out a plan and push to enable learning everywhere.

Ditch the standardization. Children are unique individuals, so it is important to create a classroom experience that will be meaningful to all regardless of expertise, support at home, abilities, interests, and so on. Different students process information in a dozen different ways—meaning they have the potential to demonstrate learning in a dozen different ways, too. In the wake of all the current high-stakes minutiae around our country, educators, politicians, and vendors should really be cognizant of tests that measure what is easy to measure but not necessarily worth measuring. Standardization matters for cholesterol and blood pressure, but does it really matter for comparative analysis of our students? We don't really use these tests to inform instruction. Why waste the money, time, and heartache on them?

Ditch the worksheets. Seriously: we've got to let these go. Drill-and-skill worksheets or workbooks do not define fluent practice, which can happen according to multiple modalities and methodologies while still being meaningful and supporting automaticity of thinking. As Marcia Tate says, "Worksheets don't grow dendrites" (2003, p. 7). There are so many more dynamic ways to engage students than resorting to instructional strategies from the 1950s.

Ditch the lecture. Storytelling is one thing; droning on and on while reading bullet points from a stale slideshow presentation is another. I'm yawning just thinking about it. (This goes for professional development, too.) Learning needs to be exciting, dynamic, and interactive, but lectures represent the lowest level of knowledge transfer and the laziest version of teaching. Unless you're Socrates or Aristotle, it's time to upgrade your operating system.

Ditch the "island mentality." In our book, *Upgrade Your Curriculum* (2013), my friend and colleague Janet Hale and I advocate for something we call "Orbits of Ability." (These are the "orbits" mentioned in the discussion of the Triptik model on p. 33.) We describe these orbits as being composed of "the knowledge and talent (expertise)" of different individuals; when they intersect and overlap, transformational things happen (p. 10). A lot of growth occurs when we allow our talents to overlap, and it saddens me to think that many teachers still operate as islands when collaboration is one of the most important skills for students to learn. Those who teach as islands are designing their own irrelevance. It is imperative that educators model the collaborative and communicative behaviors that they expect of their students.

Ditch the computer lab. In my last Arias publication, *Digital Learning Strategies* (2013), I challenged readers to "think immersive"—that is, to create immersive environments for students. This is only possible when students have tech tools available to them at all times. If you need help getting the tools, consider writing a grant—or even better, have your students write it! What an awesome opportunity for authentic learning. (For more information on securing grants, consider visiting grantwrangler.com, digitalwish.com, or donorschoose.org.)

References

Buffum, A., Mattos, M., & Weber, C. (2009). *Pyramid response to intervention*. Bloomington, IN: Solution Tree Press.

Children's Internet Protection Act. (2001). Retrieved April 27, 2015, from https://www.fcc.gov/guides/childrens-internet-protection-act

Hale, J., & Fisher, M. (2013). *Upgrade your curriculum: Practical ways to transform units and engage students*. Alexandria, VA: ASCD.

ISLLC 2008: Educational Leadership Policy Standards. (2007). Washington, DC: Council of Chief State School Officers.

Jacobs, H. (2010). *Curriculum 21: Essential education for a changing world*. Alexandria, VA: ASCD.

McTighe, J., & Wiggins, G. (2015). *Solving 25 problems in unit design: How do I refine my units to enhance student learning? (ASCD Arias)*. Alexandria, VA: ASCD.

Multidimensional Principal Performance Rubric. (2011). Available: http://lciltd.org/images/stories/PDF-files/MPPR_website.pdf

National Governor's Association Center for Best Practices & Council of Chief State School Officers. (2010). *Common Core State Standards for English Language Arts & Literacy in History/Social Studies, Science, and Technical Subjects*. Washington, DC: Authors.

National Governor's Association Center for Best Practices & Council of Chief State School Officers. (2010). *Common Core State Standards for Mathematics*. Washington, DC: Authors.

See, Think, Wonder Thinking Routine. (2014). Available: http://www.visiblethinkingpz.org/VisibleThinking_html_files/03_ThinkingRoutines/03c_Core_routines/SeeThinkWonder/SeeThink-Wonder_Routine.html

Tate, M. (2003). *Worksheets don't grow dendrites: 20 instructional strategies that engage the brain*. Thousand Oaks, CA: Corwin Press.

Texas Education Agency. (2007). Texas Essential Knowledge and Skills. Available: http://tea.texas.gov/index2.aspx?id=6148

Zmuda, A., Ullman, D., & Curtis, G. (2015). *Learning personalized: The evolution of the contemporary classroom*. San Francisco, CA: Jossey-Bass.

Acknowledgments

Extra-special thanks to those who read, reviewed, and responded with feedback at various times throughout the writing of this text. I would especially like to thank Elizabeth Fisher, Craig Gastauer, Janet Hale, Karin Pierce, Tricia Profic, Jonelle Rocke, Jessi Toepher, Diane Vigrass, and Allison Zmuda. Your insights and additional ideas were critical in helping me make this publication the best that it could be.

I would like to particularly thank Chic Foote and Cara Wolford for the depth of their editing expertise. I sincerely appreciate their wisdom and their willingness to give quick and meaningful feedback.

Thanks to Genny Ostertag at ASCD. Yet again, you listened to me ramble on with my nebulous thoughts and somehow extracted the best ideas.

Thanks to Ernesto Yermoli, editor extraordinaire. I'm thrilled to be able to work with you again and look forward to many more projects together.

And finally, thank you to my children, Lily and Charlotte. You're so patient when I'm on the computer, and I promise: we're leaving for the park in five more minutes!

Related Resources

At the time of publication, the following ASCD resources were available (ASCD stock numbers appear in parentheses). For up-to-date information about ASCD resources, go to www.ascd.org.

ASCD EDge®
Exchange ideas and connect with other educators interested in planning for meaningful student learning on the social networking site ASCD EDge® at http://ascdedge.ascd.org.

Freedom to Fail: How do I foster risk-taking and innovation in my classroom? (ASCD Arias) by Andrew K. Miller (#SF115044)

Getting Started with Blended Learning: How do I integrate online and face-to-face instruction? (ASCD Arias) by William Kist (#SF115073)

Solving 25 Problems in Unit Design: How do I refine my units to enhance student learning? (ASCD Arias) by Jay McTighe and Grant Wiggins (#SF115046)

Authentic Learning in the Digital Age: Engaging Students Through Inquiry by Larissa Pahomov (#115009)

Productive Group Work: How To Engage Students, Build Teamwork, And Promote Understanding by Nancy Frey, Douglas Fisher, and Sandi Everlove (#109018)

ASCD PD Online Courses
Project-Based Learning: An Answer To The Common Core Challenge (#PD13OC008M)
Teach, Reflect, Learn: Building Your Capacity For Success In The Classroom (#PD15OC004M)

About the Author

Michael Fisher is an instructional coach and educational consultant specializing in the intersection between instructional technology and curriculum design. He works with districts across the country helping teachers and schools maximize available technology, software, and Web-based resources while attending to curriculum design, instructional practices, and assessments. He posts frequently at ASCD EDge (edge.ascd.org), the Curriculum 21 blog (www.curriculum21.com/blog), and his own blog (digigogy. blogspot.com). He's written two previous books for ASCD, *Upgrade Your Curriculum: Practical Ways to Transform Units and Engage Students,* with co-author Janet Hale, and *Digital Learning Strategies: How do I assign and assess 21st century work?* (ASCD Arias). You can contact him via email at digigogy@gmail.com or by visiting his website at www. digigogy.com.

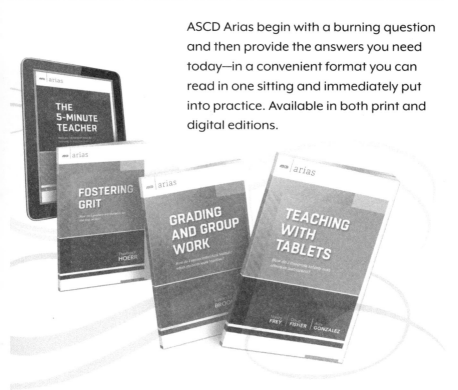